100 Genealogy & Family History Tips

MELISSA DICKERSON,
GENEALOGY GIRL TALKS

Copyright © 2017 Genealogy Girl Talks / RMJET, LLC

All rights reserved.

ISBN:1981508635
ISBN-13: 978-1981508631

DEDICATION

This book is dedicated to all those who have encouraged me in my pursuit of Family History research and writing.

CONTENTS

Introduction

What started as a 100 Day Project for me has now become a book. It was during 2017 that I learned about the 100 Day Project. A project that encourages participants to do one thing creatively for 100 days. Naturally, I decided to create something related to Genealogy & Family History. That is how these 100 Genealogy Tip were envisioned.

Some are educational, some are inspirational, but all are Family History & Genealogy related.

I hope they help you in your own research journey…

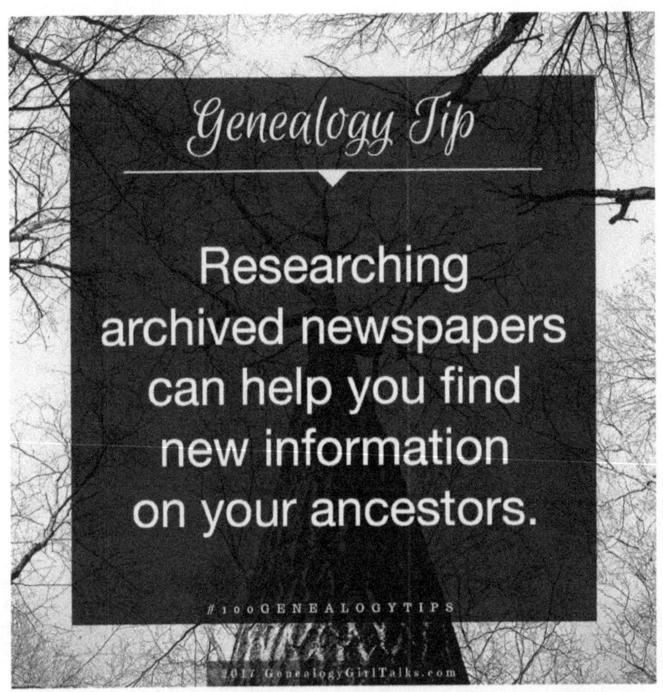
Genealogy Tip

Researching
archived newspapers
can help you find
new information
on your ancestors.

#100GENEALOGYTIPS

2017 GenealogyGirlTalks.com

Genealogy Tip

Timelines are a great way
to view your ancestor's life.
They also let you see
any gaps in your research.

#100GENEALOGYTIPS

©2017 GenealogyGirlTalks.com

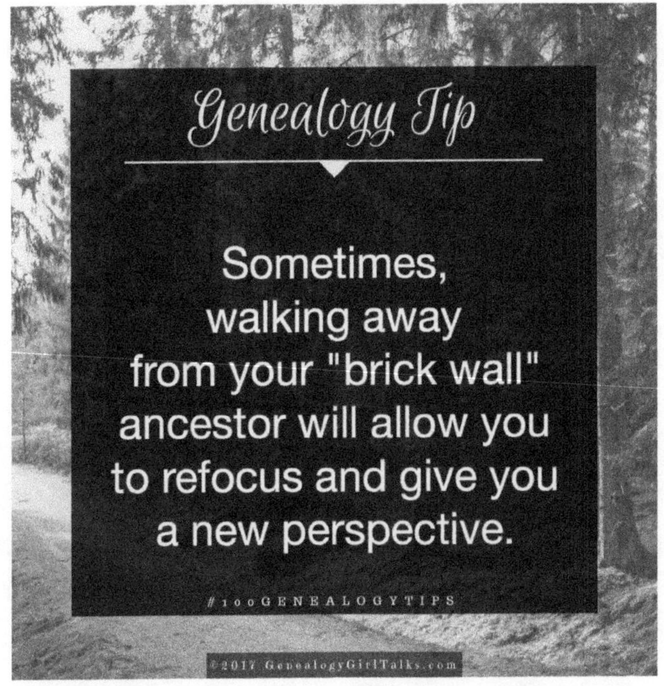
Genealogy Tip

Sometimes,
walking away
from your "brick wall"
ancestor will allow you
to refocus and give you
a new perspective.

#100GENEALOGYTIPS

©2017 GenealogyGirlTalks.com

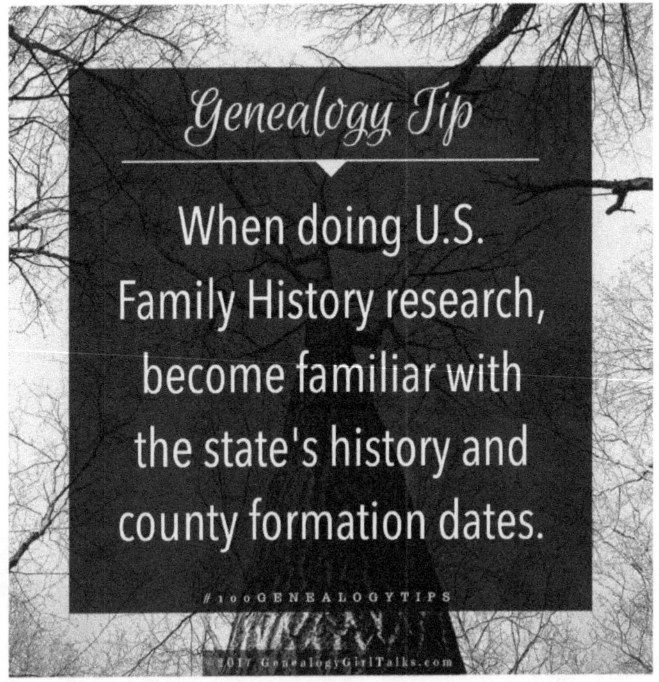
Genealogy Tip

When doing U.S. Family History research, become familiar with the state's history and county formation dates.

#100GENEALOGYTIPS

2017 GenealogyGirlTalks.com

05. Start With Yourself

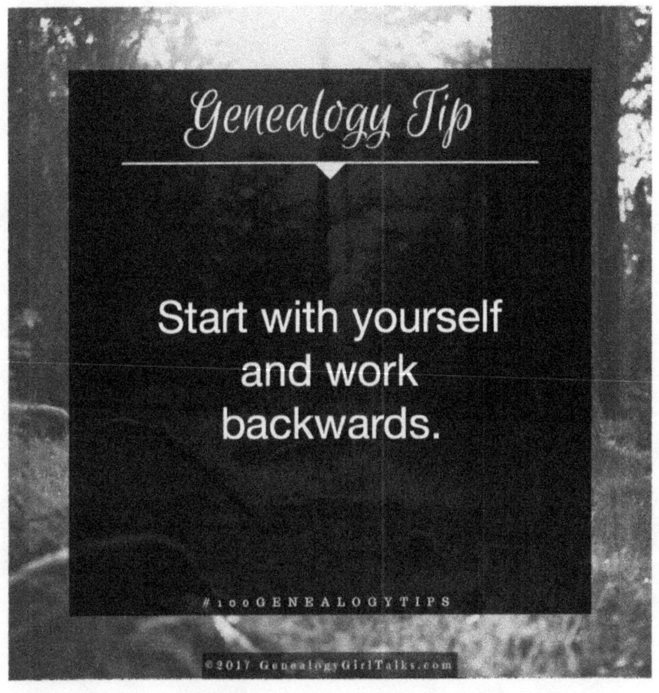

Genealogy Tip
If you are starting a family history blog, remember to keep your blog's name simple, make it memorable, and select a searchable name.
#100GENEALOGYTIPS
©2017 GenealogyGirlTalks.com

07. Use Hashtags

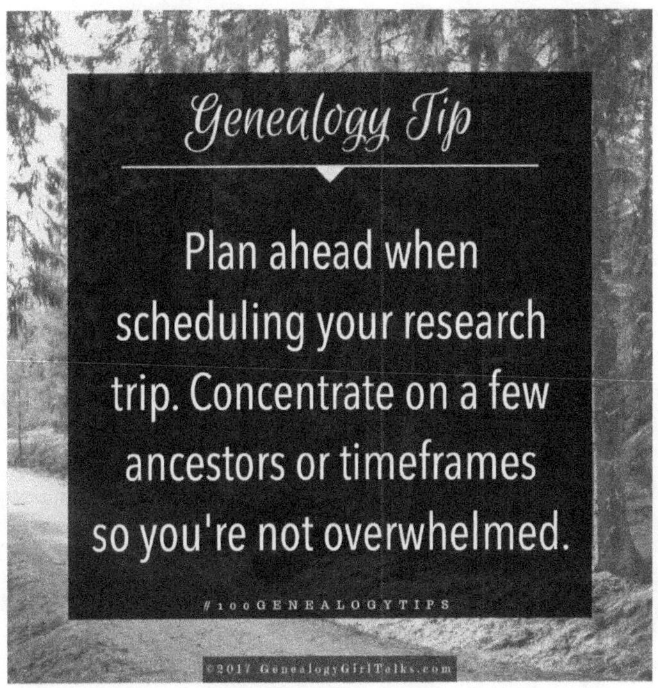

Genealogy Tip

Plan ahead when scheduling your research trip. Concentrate on a few ancestors or timeframes so you're not overwhelmed.

#100GENEALOGYTIPS

©2017 GenealogyGirlTalks.com

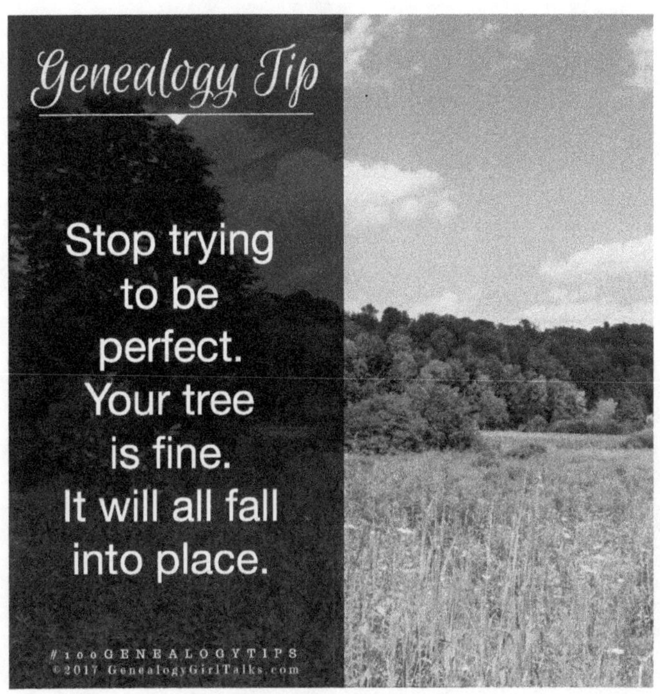
Genealogy Tip

Stop trying
to be
perfect.
Your tree
is fine.
It will all fall
into place.

#100GENEALOGYTIPS
©2017 GenealogyGirlTalks.com

Genealogy Tip
Listen closely to oral history.
#100GENEALOGYTIPS
©2017 GenealogyGirlTalks.com

22

Genealogy Tip

When using Pinterest
for your Family History,
name your boards
with family surnames.
This will make them easier
for others to find.

#100GENEALOGYTIPS
2017 GenealogyGirlTalks.com

12. INSTAGRAM

25

13. INTERACT WITH OTHERS

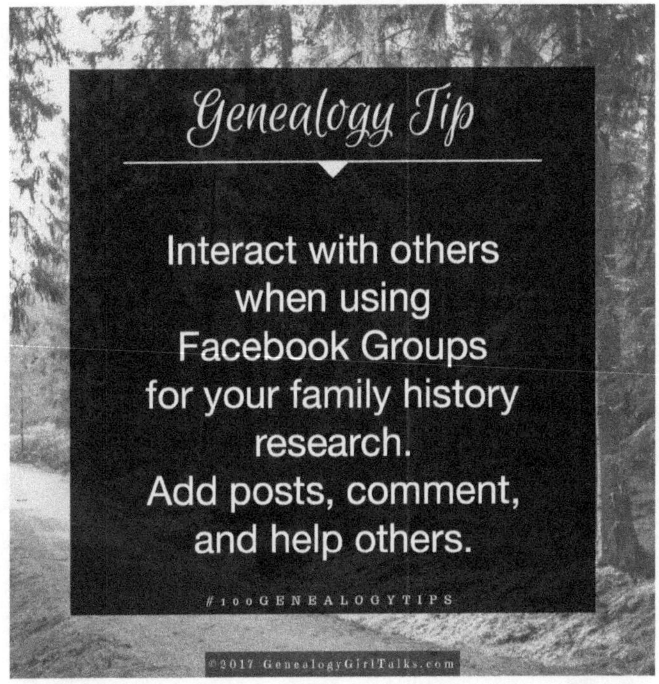

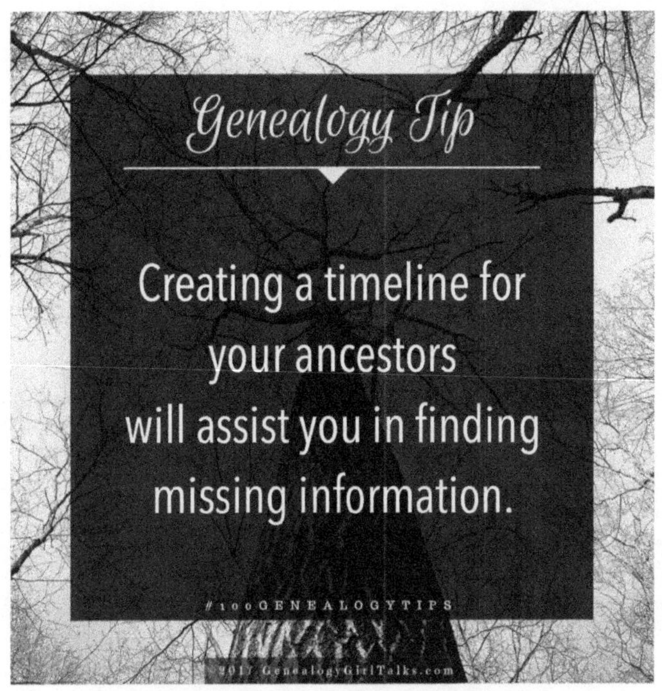
Genealogy Tip

Creating a timeline for
your ancestors
will assist you in finding
missing information.

#100GENEALOGYTIPS

2017 GenealogyGirlTalks.com

Genealogy Tip

When doing
Google searches,
include your
ancestor's name
and location.

#100GENEALOGYTIPS

©2017 GenealogyGirlTalks.com

Genealogy Tip

When you encounter
a brickwall ancestor,
research their siblings.
You may find more clues
in their records.

#100GENEALOGYTIPS

©2017 GenealogyGirlTalks.com

17. TAKE SMALL STEPS

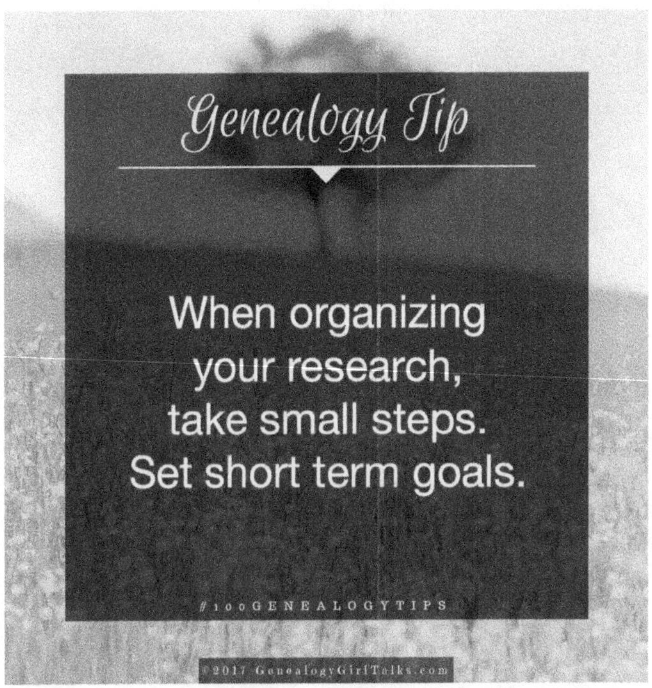

18. GOOGLE BOOKS

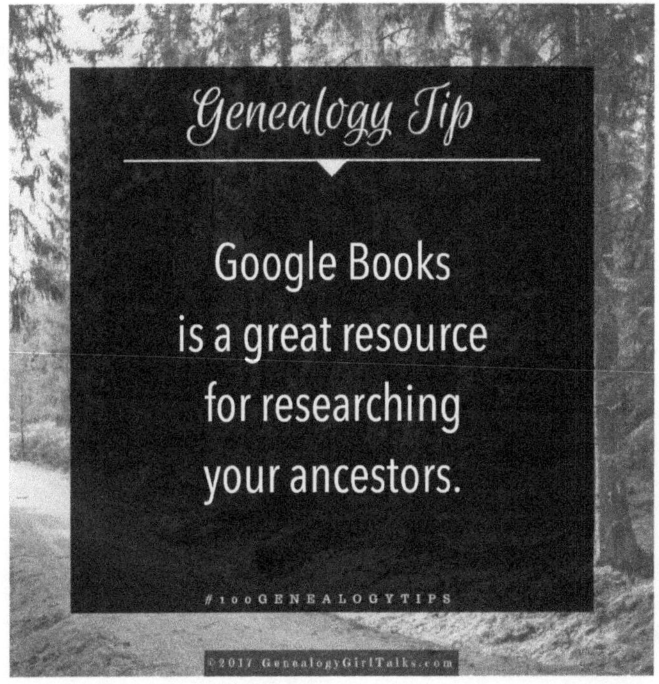

19. Check The Neighbors

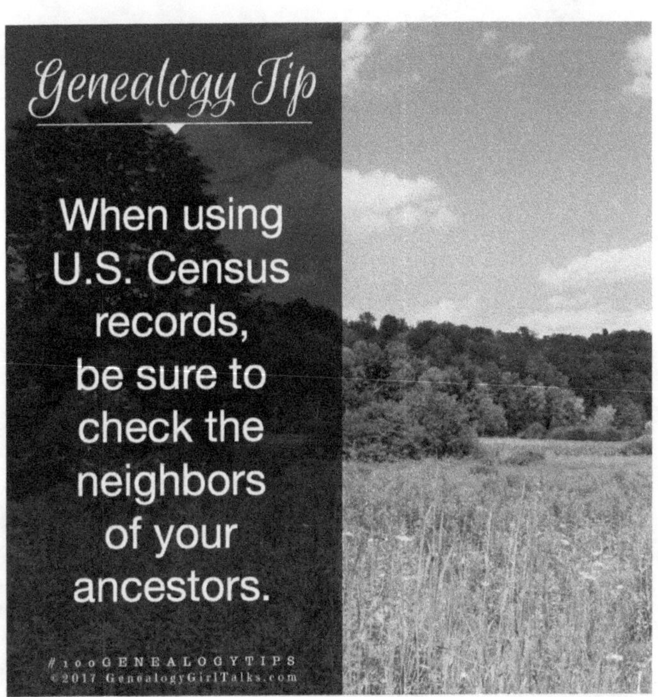

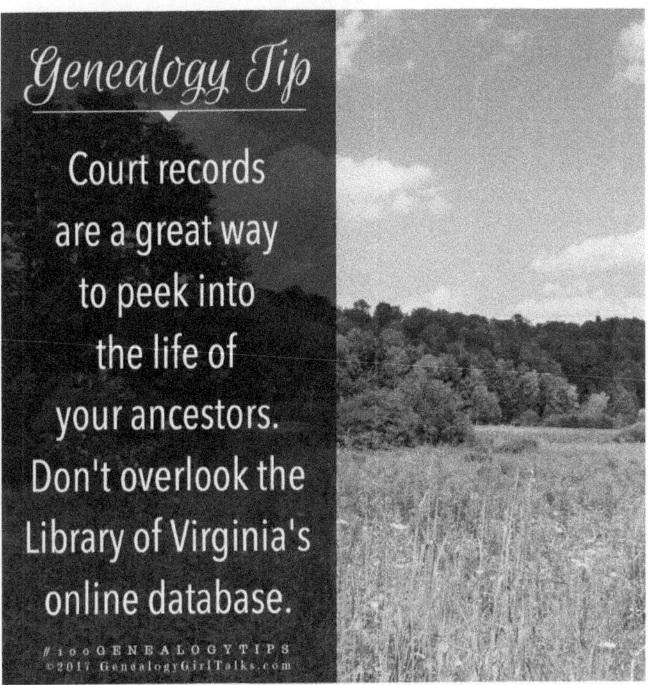

Genealogy Tip
Court records
are a great way
to peek into
the life of
your ancestors.
Don't overlook the
Library of Virginia's
online database.
#100GENEALOGYTIPS
©2017 GenealogyGirlTalks.com

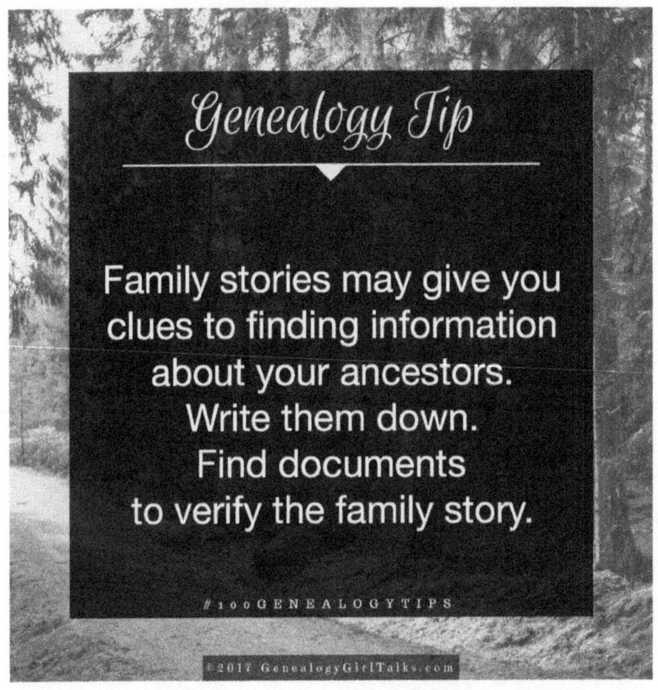
Genealogy Tip

Family stories may give you
clues to finding information
about your ancestors.
Write them down.
Find documents
to verify the family story.

#100GENEALOGYTIPS

©2017 GenealogyGirlTalks.com

22. Go Slow

Genealogy Tip

Family History research
is not a race.
Go slow,
verify your information,
and have fun!

#100GENEALOGYTIPS

©2017 GenealogyGirlTalks.com

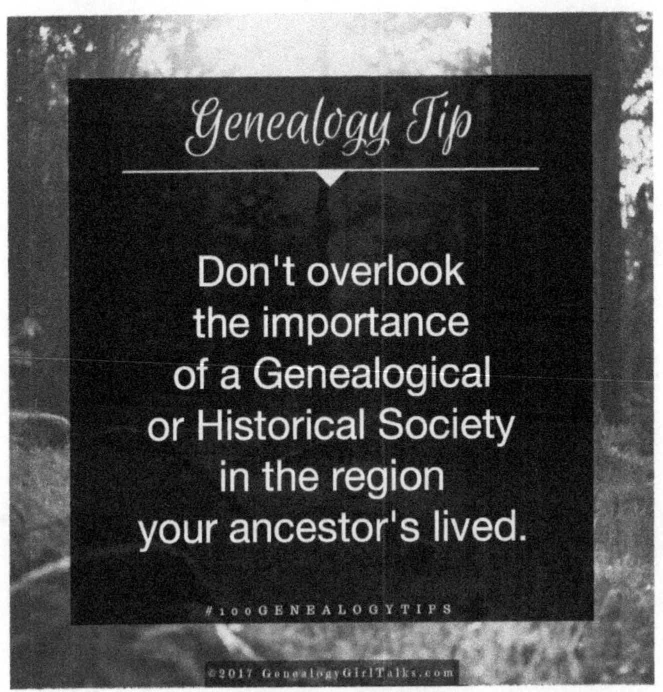
Genealogy Tip

Don't overlook
the importance
of a Genealogical
or Historical Society
in the region
your ancestor's lived.

#100GENEALOGYTIPS

©2017 GenealogyGirlTalks.com

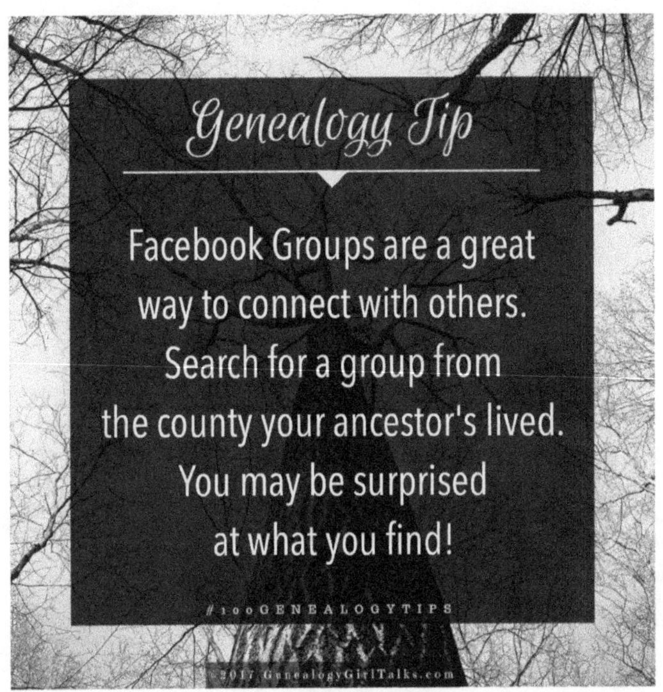

Genealogy Tip

Facebook Groups are a great
way to connect with others.
Search for a group from
the county your ancestor's lived.
You may be surprised
at what you find!

#100GENEALOGYTIPS

2017 GenealogyGirlTalks.com

Genealogy Tip
Sometimes disproving a theory is just as important as proving one.
#100GENEALOGYTIPS
©2017 GenealogyGirlTalks.com

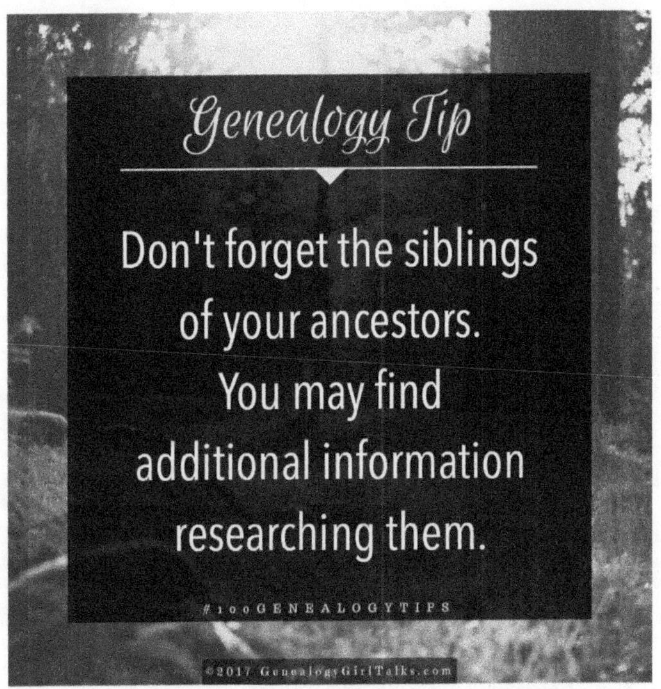

Genealogy Tip

Don't forget the siblings
of your ancestors.
You may find
additional information
researching them.

#100GENEALOGYTIPS

©2017 GenealogyGirlTalks.com

27. LEARN THEIR LIVES

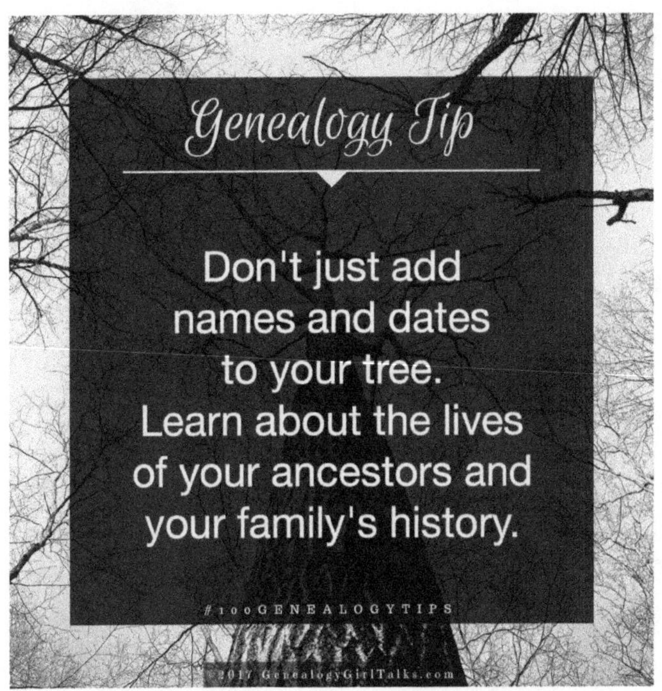

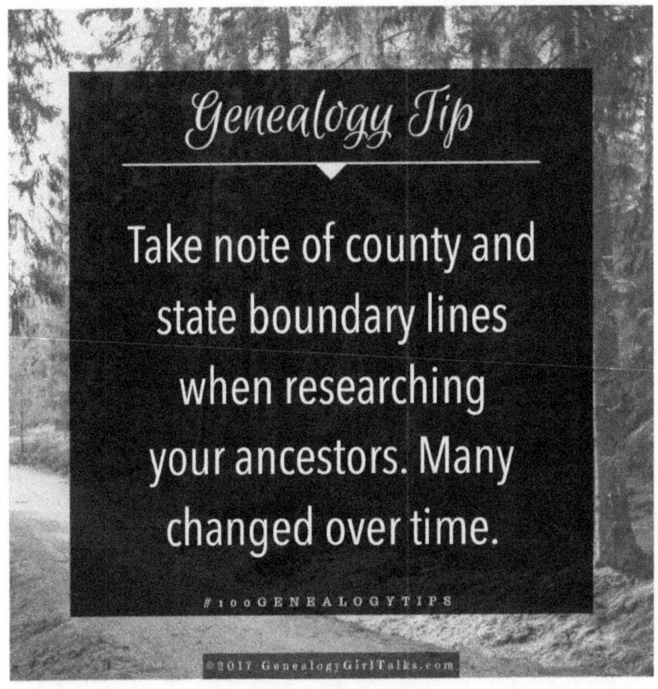
Genealogy Tip

Take note of county and
state boundary lines
when researching
your ancestors. Many
changed over time.

#100GENEALOGYTIPS

©2017 GenealogyGirlTalks.com

29. Use Credible Websites

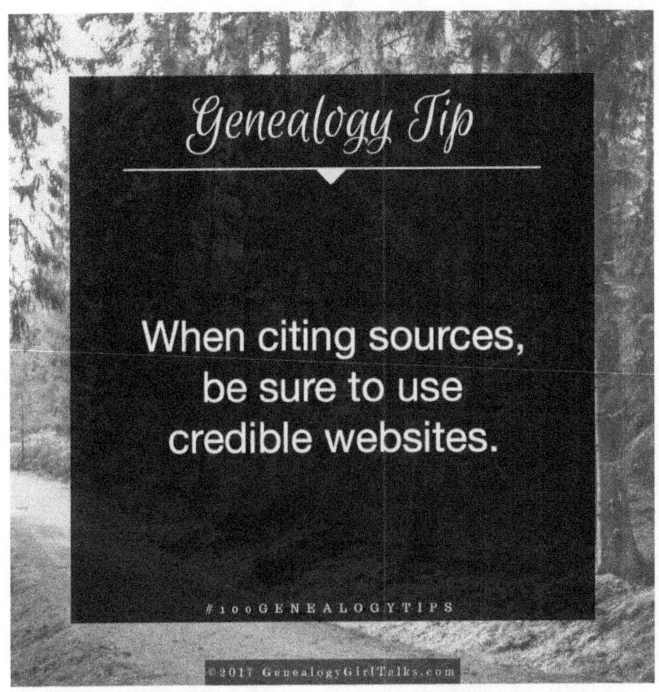

Genealogy Tip

Don't overlook
smaller family
trees on Ancestry.
Some of them
are based
on firsthand
knowledge.

#100GENEALOGYTIPS
©2017 GenealogyGirlTalks.com

31. CHECK SPELLINGS

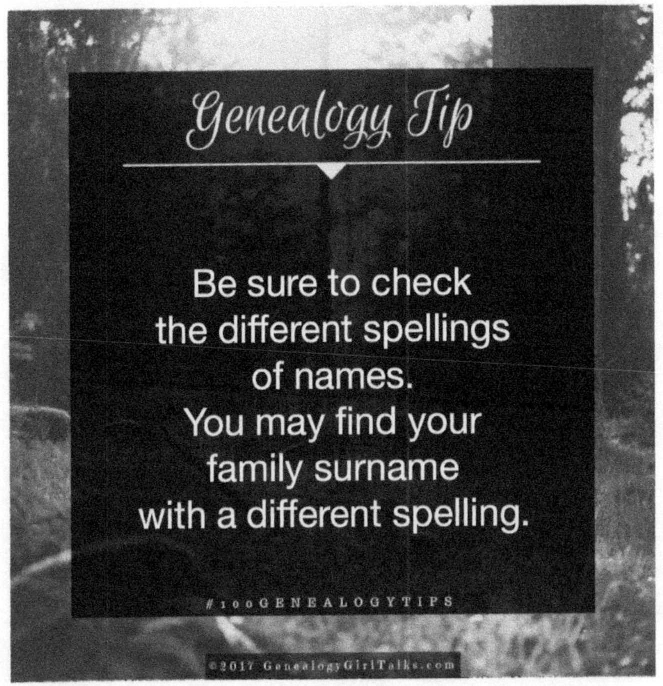

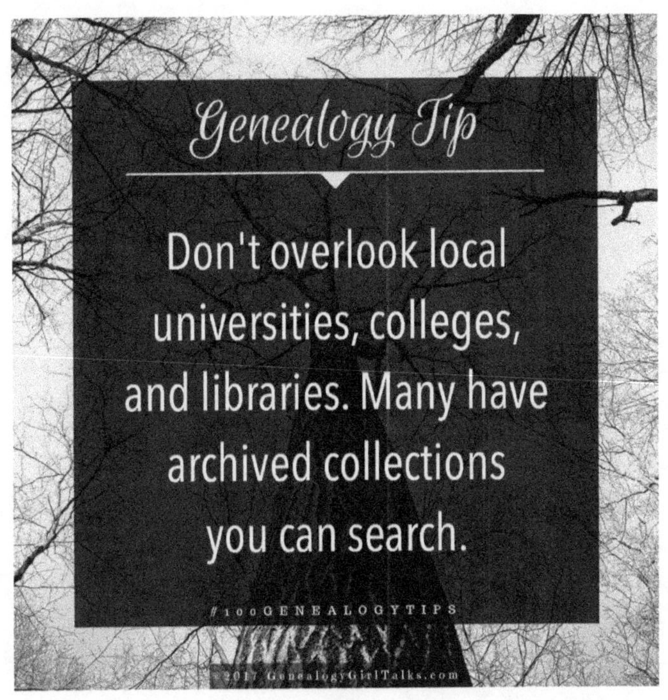
Genealogy Tip

Don't overlook local universities, colleges, and libraries. Many have archived collections you can search.

#100GENEALOGYTIPS

2017 GenealogyGirlTalks.com

Genealogy Tip

Twitter's list feature
can help you organize
the users you follow.
Create a list to sort them
by topic. You can even
make private lists
that only you can see!

#100GENEALOGYTIPS

©2017 GenealogyGirlTalks.com

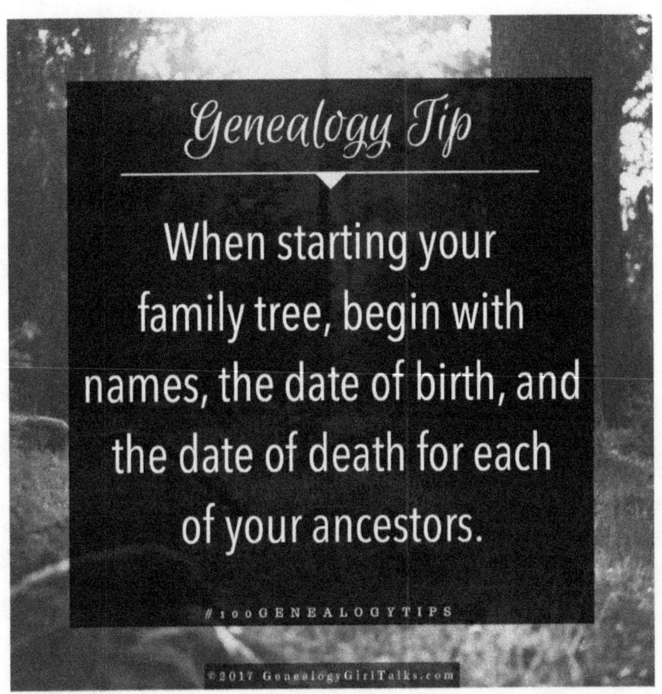
Genealogy Tip

When starting your family tree, begin with names, the date of birth, and the date of death for each of your ancestors.

#100GENEALOGYTIPS

©2017 GenealogyGirlTalks.com

Genealogy Tip

Start with
a family story.
Research
newspapers,
archives, records,
and documents
to confirm
or deny the story.

#100GENEALOGYTIPS
©2017 GenealogyGirlTalks.com

36. USING PINTEREST

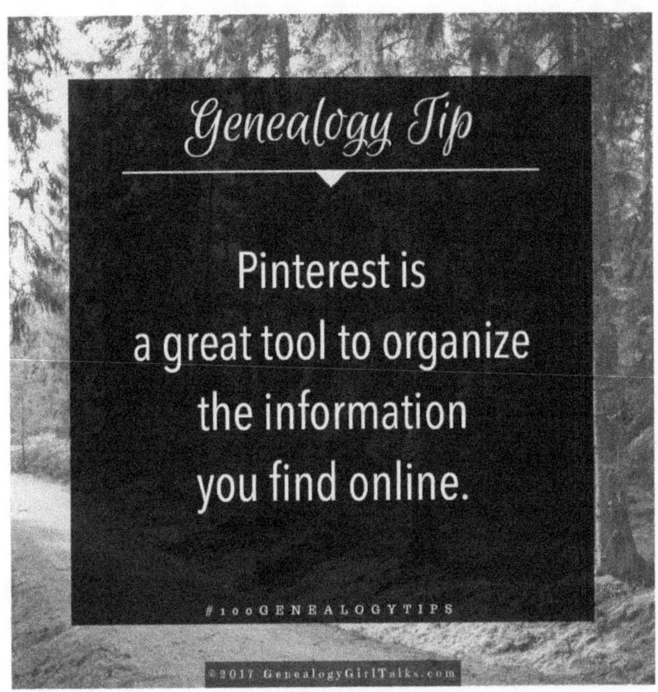

Genealogy Tip

Keep a research journal.
Document the steps
you took to find
your information,
where you located records,
and your next steps.

#100GENEALOGYTIPS

©2017 GenealogyGirlTalks.com

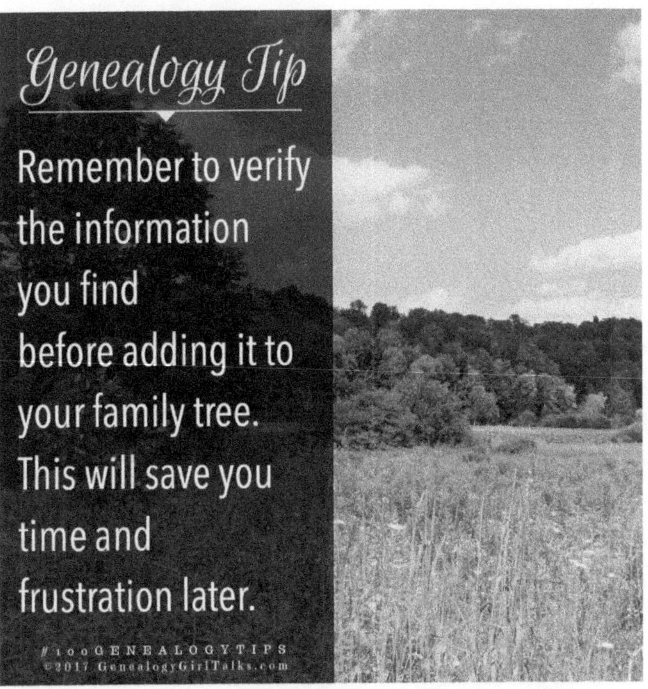
Genealogy Tip

Remember to verify
the information
you find
before adding it to
your family tree.
This will save you
time and
frustration later.

#100GENEALOGYTIPS
©2017 GenealogyGirlTalks.com

39. Census Records

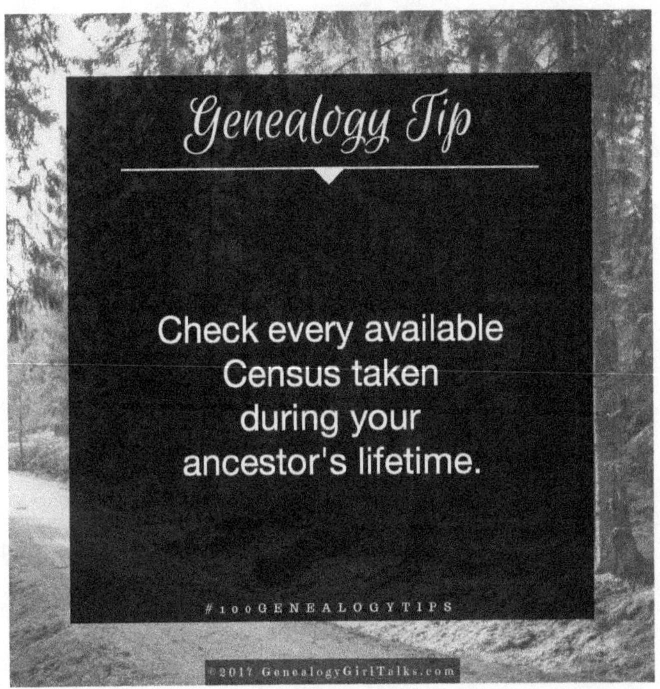

40. Cite Your Sources

41. TWITTER CHATS

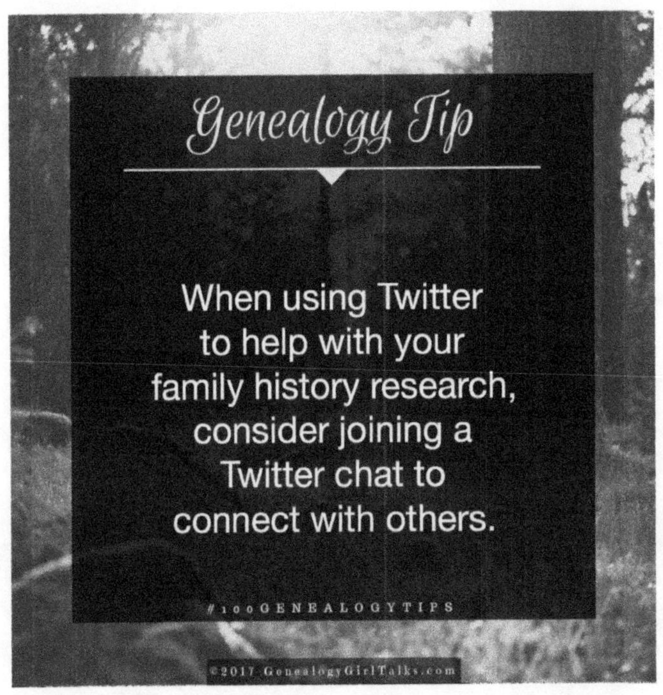

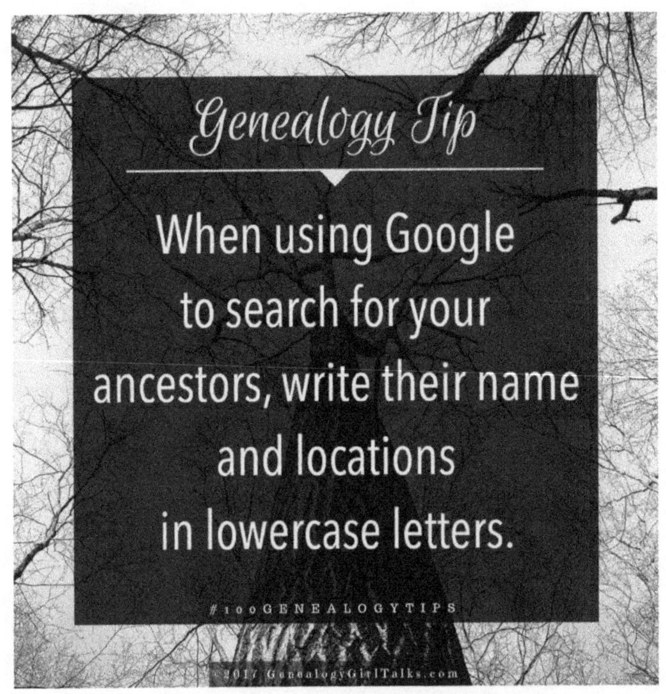
Genealogy Tip

When using Google
to search for your
ancestors, write their name
and locations
in lowercase letters.

#100GENEALOGYTIPS

©2017 GenealogyGirlTalks.com

43. Unique Names

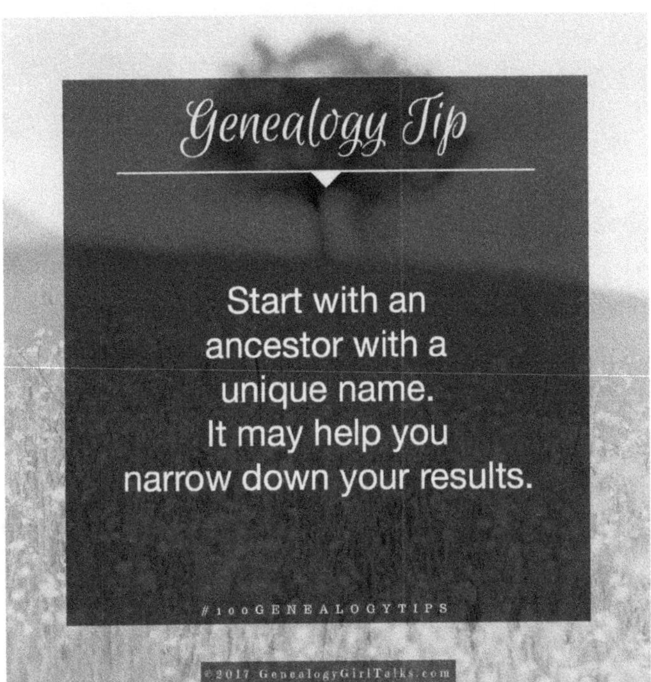

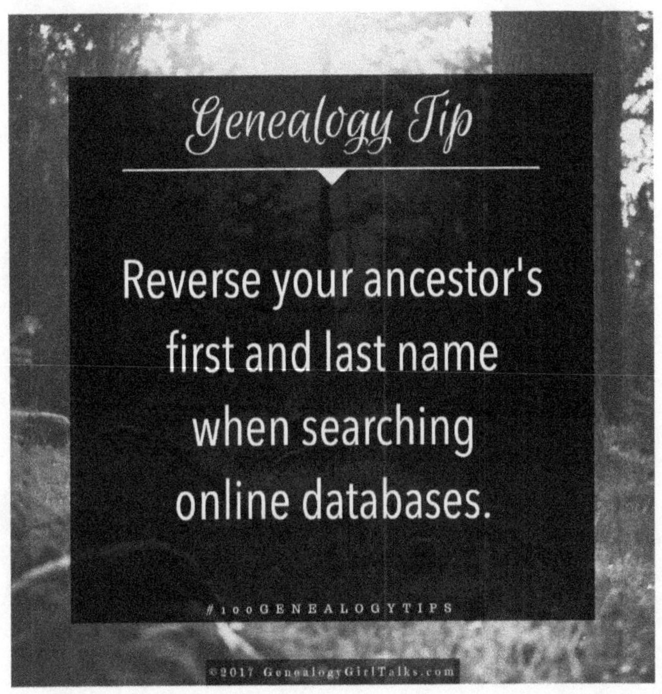
Genealogy Tip
Reverse your ancestor's first and last name when searching online databases.
#100GENEALOGYTIPS
©2017 GenealogyGirlTalks.com

Genealogy Tip

Use
wildcards
when doing
online
searches.

#100GENEALOGYTIPS
©2017 GenealogyGirlTalks.com

46. COUNTRY SPECIFIC

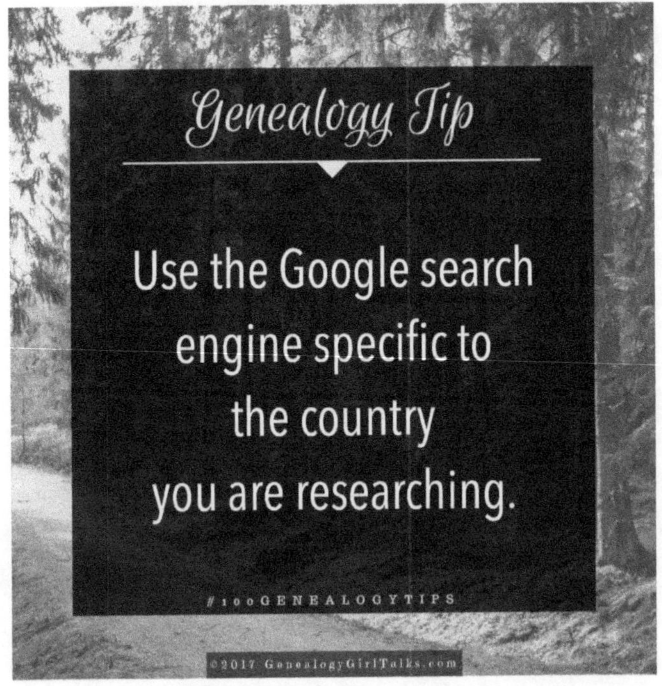

Genealogy Tip

Don't give up!
Sometimes you
will find
what you're looking for
when you least expect it!

#100GENEALOGYTIPS

2017 GenealogyGirlTalks.com

Genealogy Tip

Become familiar
with first name
abbreviations
when searching
old records
and documents.

#100GENEALOGYTIPS
©2017 GenealogyGirlTalks.com

49. MOBILE APPS

Genealogy Tip

Remember to add
a watermark to
your family photographs.

#100GENEALOGYTIPS

©2017 GenealogyGirlTalks.com

Genealogy Tip
Don't overlook
Google's
Advanced Search
feature.
#100GENEALOGYTIPS
©2017 GenealogyGirlTalks.com

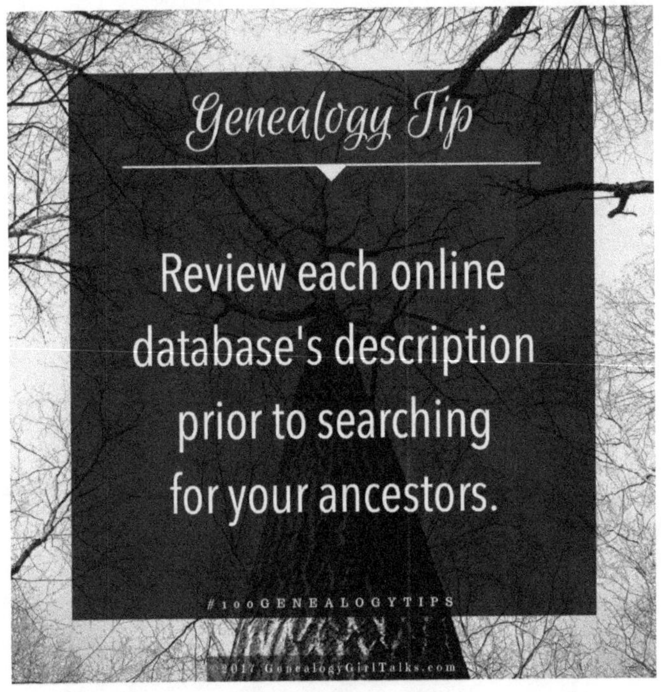
Genealogy Tip

Review each online
database's description
prior to searching
for your ancestors.

#100GENEALOGYTIPS
2017 GenealogyGirlTalks.com

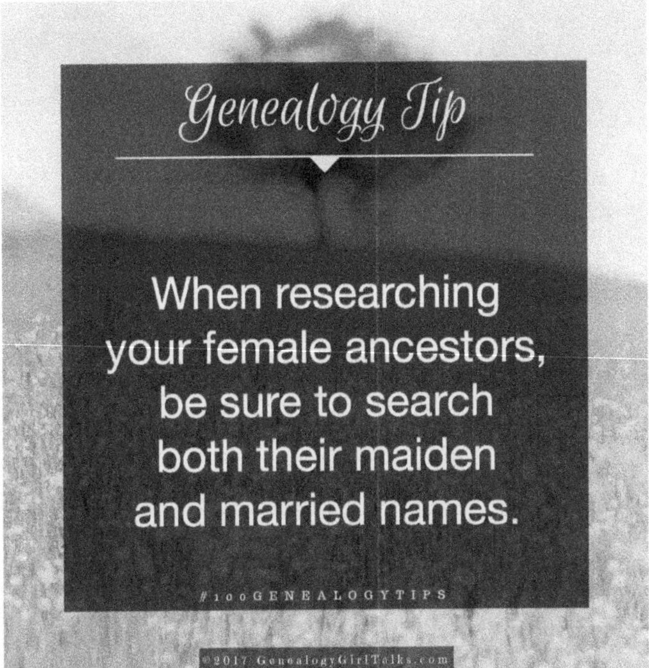
Genealogy Tip

When researching
your female ancestors,
be sure to search
both their maiden
and married names.

#100GENEALOGYTIPS

©2017 GenealogyGirlTalks.com

54. Less Is More

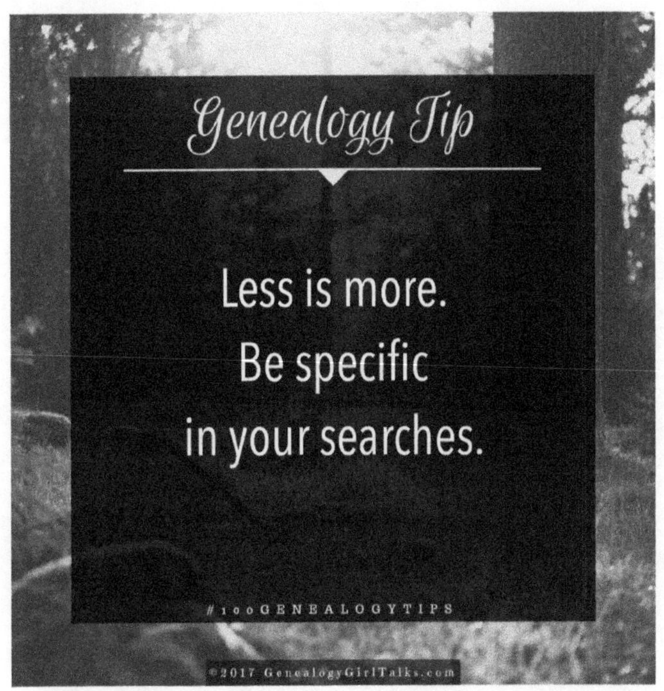

Genealogy Tip

Database and
record
indexes
are only guides.
They are
not credible
sources.

#100GENEALOGYTIPS
©2017 GenealogyGirlTalks.com

Genealogy Tip

Narrow your searches
with the date range
when using Google's
Advanced Search feature.

#100GENEALOGYTIPS

©2017 GenealogyGirlTalks.com

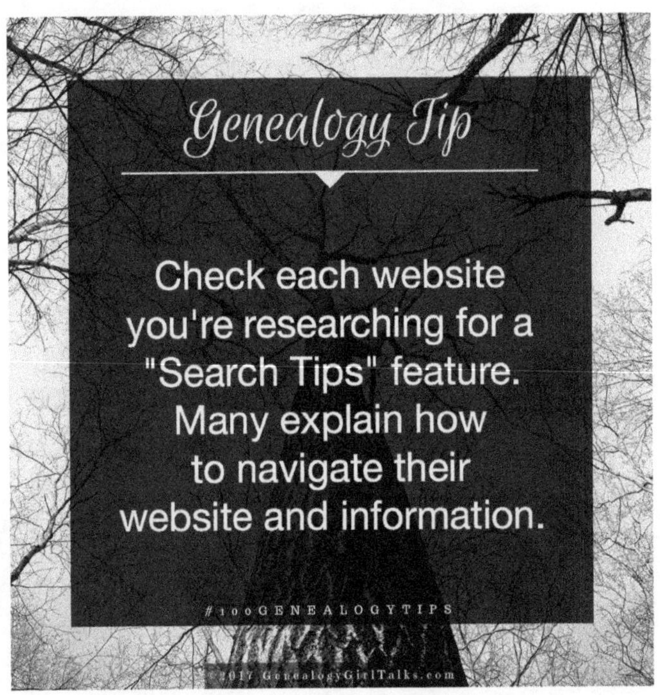

Genealogy Tip

Check each website
you're researching for a
"Search Tips" feature.
Many explain how
to navigate their
website and information.

#100GENEALOGYTIPS

2017 GenealogyGirlTalks.com

Genealogy Tip
Start your
searches
as narrow
as possible.
Slowly broaden
your parameters.
#100GENEALOGYTIPS
©2017 GenealogyGirlTalks.com

Genealogy Tip

Consider microblogging
to share your family history
and family photographs.
Platforms like Instagram,
Facebook, Twitter,
and more are great places!

#100GENEALOGYTIPS

©2017 GenealogyGirlTalks.com

60. Use Quotation Marks

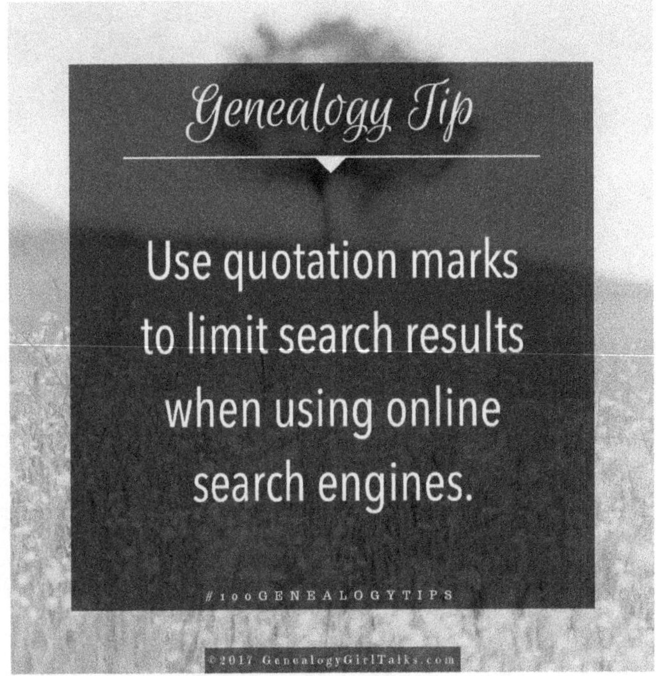

Genealogy Tip

Most libraries have a
Genealogy section
you can research.
You may find information
on surrounding counties
and even early settlers
of the region.

#100GENEALOGYTIPS

©2017 GenealogyGirlTalks.com

Genealogy Tip

Church records
hold valuable
information.

#100GENEALOGYTIPS

©2017 GenealogyGirlTalks.com

Genealogy Tip

When using social media
to connect with others and
research your family history,
be sure to complete
your profile.
This will help others find you.

#100GENEALOGYTIPS

©2017 GenealogyGirlTalks.com

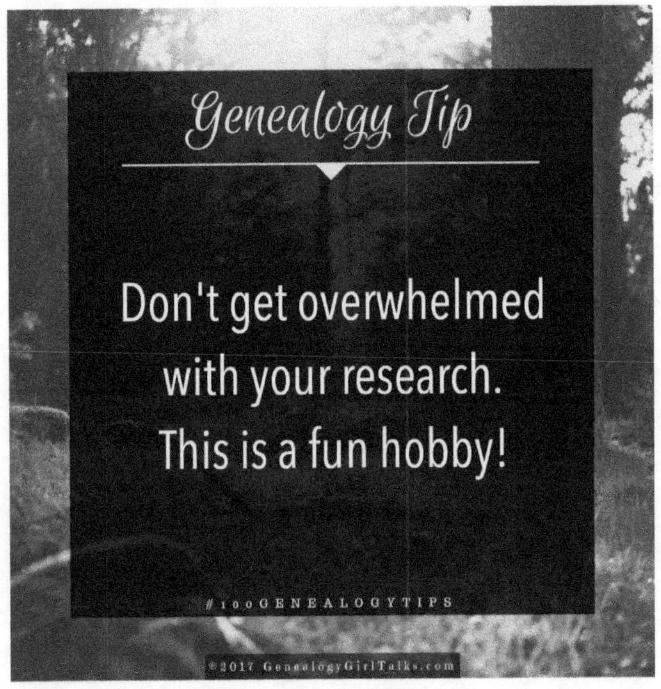
Genealogy Tip

Don't get overwhelmed
with your research.
This is a fun hobby!

#100GENEALOGYTIPS

©2017 GenealogyGirlTalks.com

65. GO SIDEWAYS

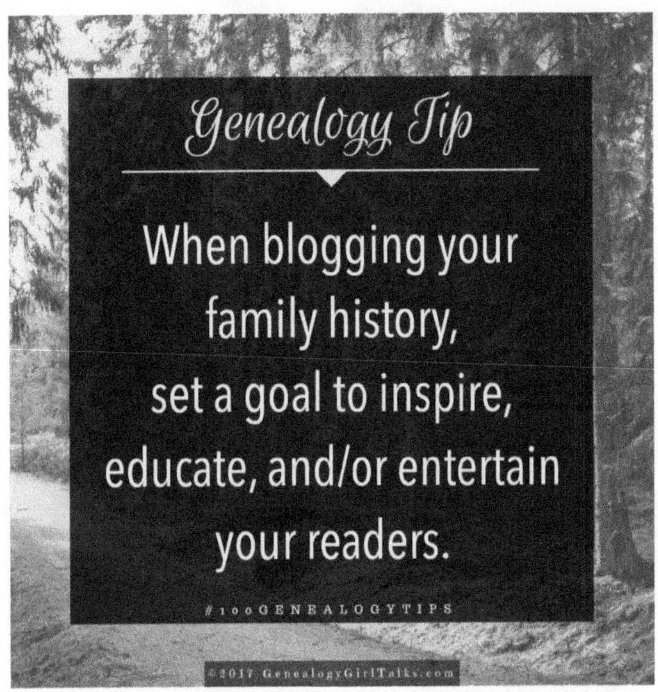
Genealogy Tip

When blogging your
family history,
set a goal to inspire,
educate, and/or entertain
your readers.

#100GENEALOGYTIPS

©2017 GenealogyGirlTalks.com

67. Pinterest Boards

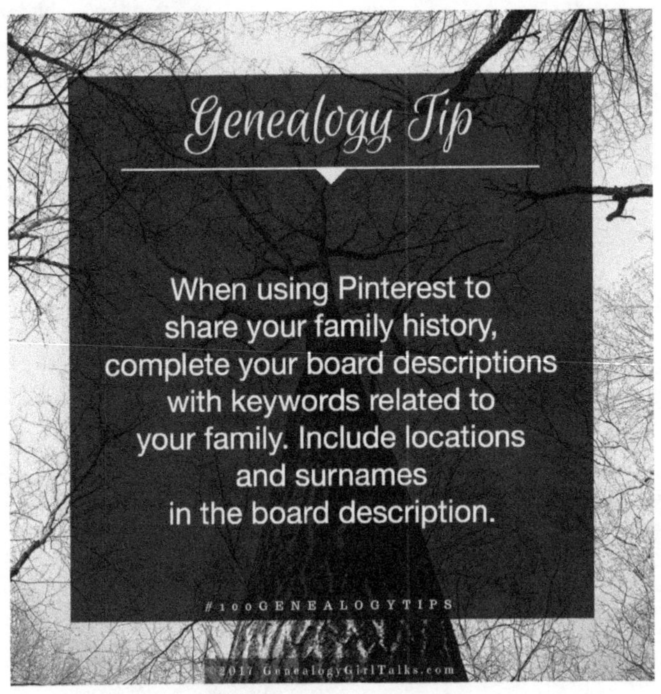

Genealogy Tip

Kindness matters.
Be kind to others
when sharing,
commenting,
and interacting
with others
online.

#100GENEALOGYTIPS
©2017 GenealogyGirlTalks.com

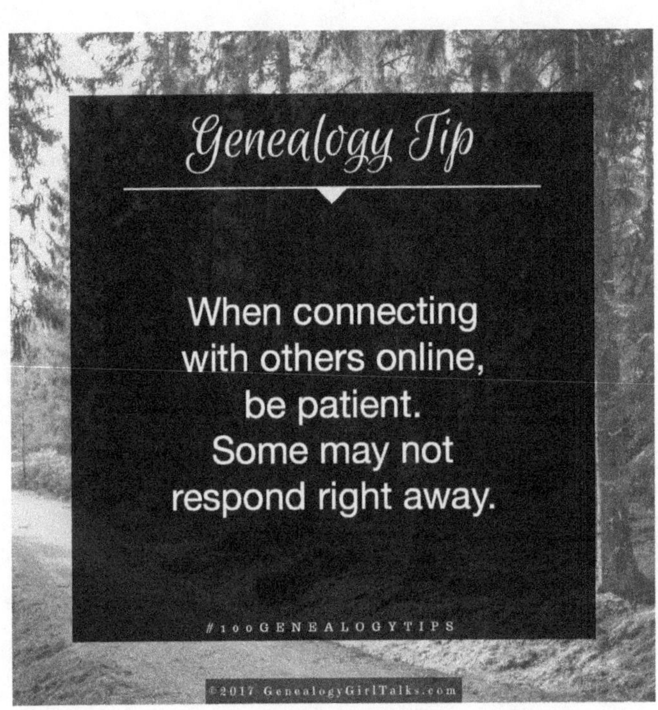

Genealogy Tip

When connecting
with others online,
be patient.
Some may not
respond right away.

#100GENEALOGYTIPS

©2017 GenealogyGirlTalks.com

Genealogy Tip

Pinterest is
a great way to connect
with family and
share your research.

#100GENEALOGYTIPS

©2017 GenealogyGirlTalks.com

71. SURNAME GROUPS

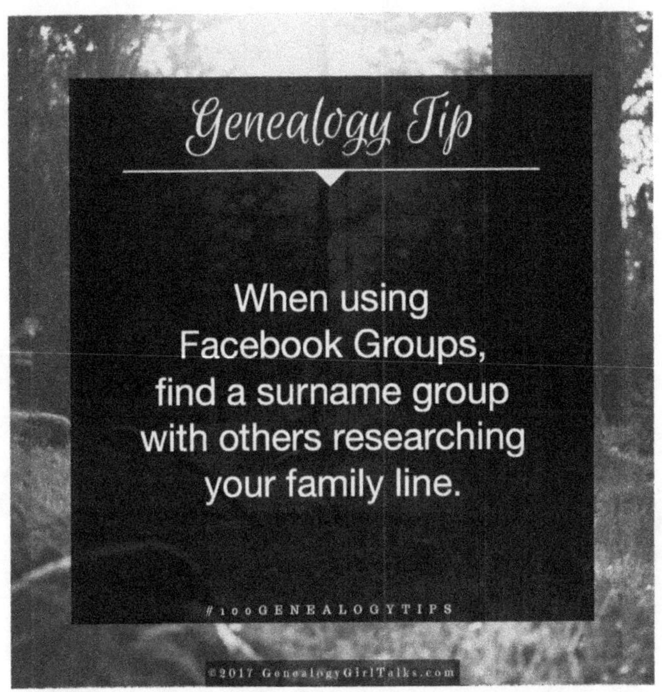

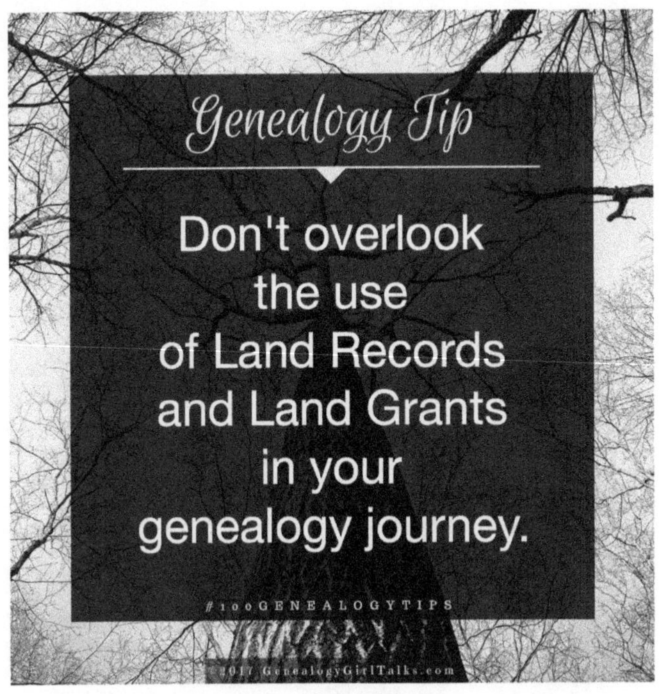
Genealogy Tip

Don't overlook
the use
of Land Records
and Land Grants
in your
genealogy journey.

#100GENEALOGYTIPS

2017 GenealogyGirlTalks.com

Genealogy Tip
When is the right time
to start your
family history blog?
Now. Now is the right time.
#100GENEALOGYTIPS
©2017 GenealogyGirlTalks.com

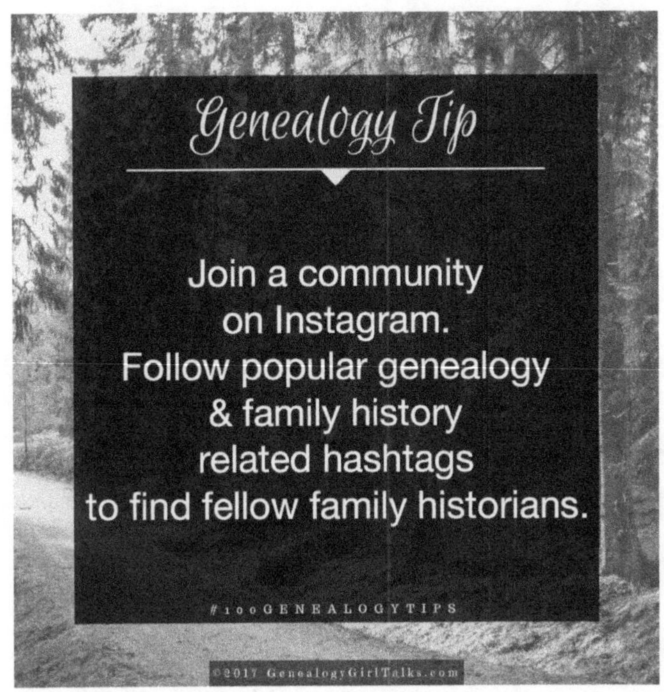
Genealogy Tip

Join a community
on Instagram.
Follow popular genealogy
& family history
related hashtags
to find fellow family historians.

#100GENEALOGYTIPS

©2017 GenealogyGirlTalks.com

Genealogy Tip

Research
one ancestor
at a time.
You'll
get there!

#100GENEALOGYTIPS
©2017 GenealogyGirlTalks.com

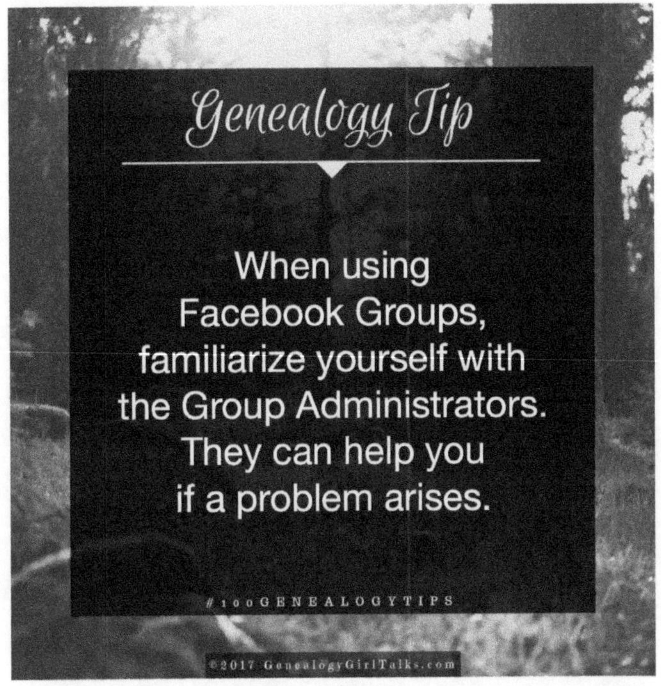
Genealogy Tip

When using
Facebook Groups,
familiarize yourself with
the Group Administrators.
They can help you
if a problem arises.

#100GENEALOGYTIPS

©2017 GenealogyGirlTalks.com

Genealogy Tip

Create "Memorial" boards
on Pinterest for your
ancestors and loved ones.
Include their favorite items,
things they loved,
places they visited, and more.

#100GENEALOGYTIPS

2017 GenealogyGirlTalks.com

78. It Never Ends

Genealogy Tip

Get out of your comfort zone.
Research a new way.
Find a new angle.
Find new records to research.

#100GENEALOGYTIPS

©2017 GenealogyGirlTalks.com

Genealogy Tip
When using
Instagram,
share photos
from your
local area/region.
This will help others
learn the history
of the area
their ancestors lived.
#100GENEALOGYTIPS
©2017 GenealogyGirlTalks.com

81. CHECK THE PAGES

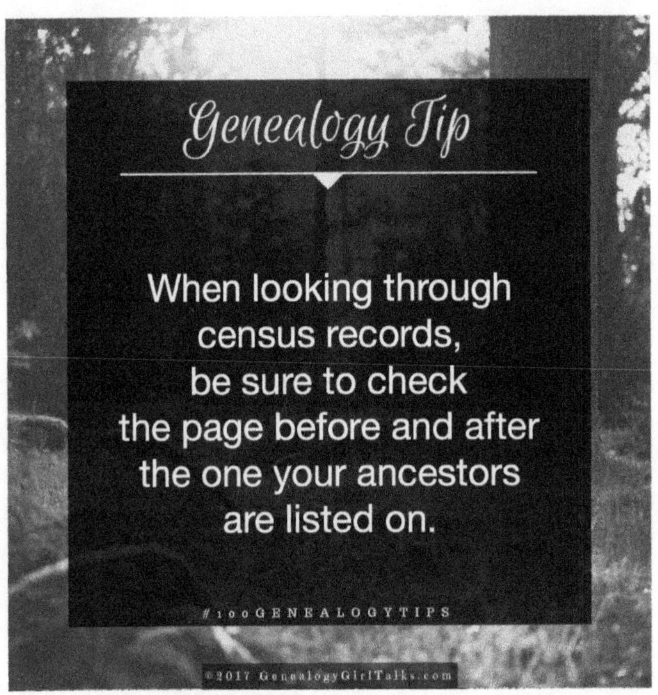

82. SAVE DOCUMENTS

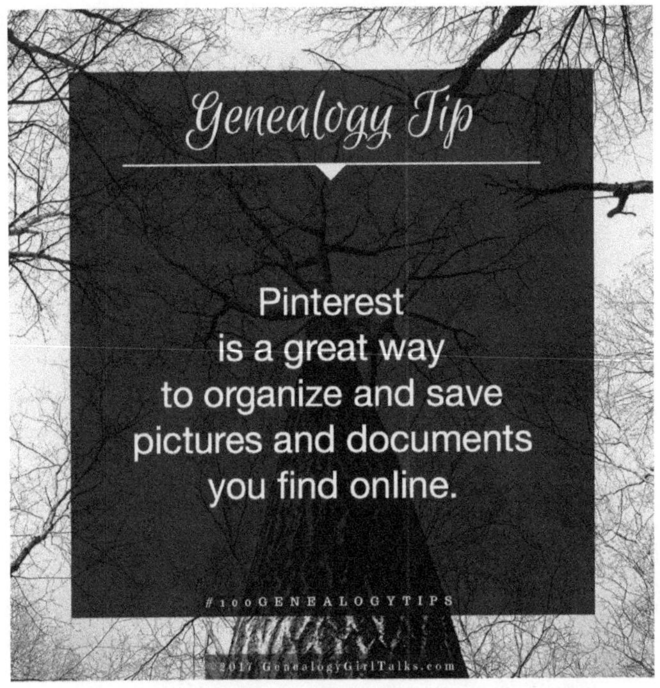

Genealogy Tip
Don't
make
assumptions.
#100GENEALOGYTIPS
©2017 GenealogyGirlTalks.com

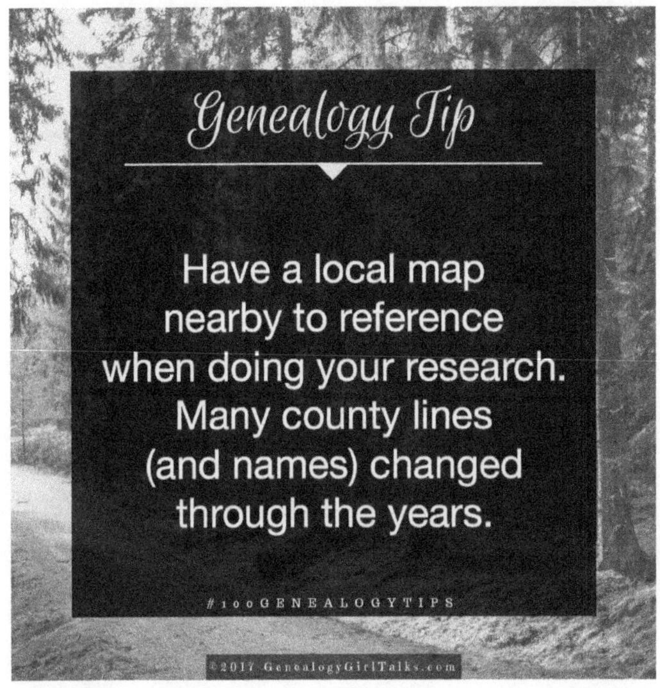
Genealogy Tip

Have a local map
nearby to reference
when doing your research.
Many county lines
(and names) changed
through the years.

#100GENEALOGYTIPS

©2017 GenealogyGirlTalks.com

Genealogy Tip

Facebook Groups
are a great way
to share your findings
with family. If you don't see
a Group you like,
create your own!

#100GENEALOGYTIPS
2017 GenealogyGirlTalks.com

86. Free Charts & Forms

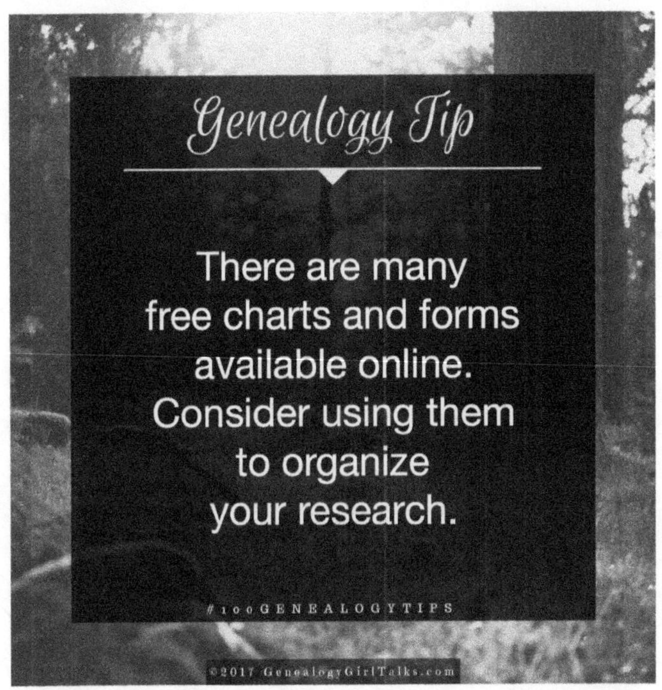

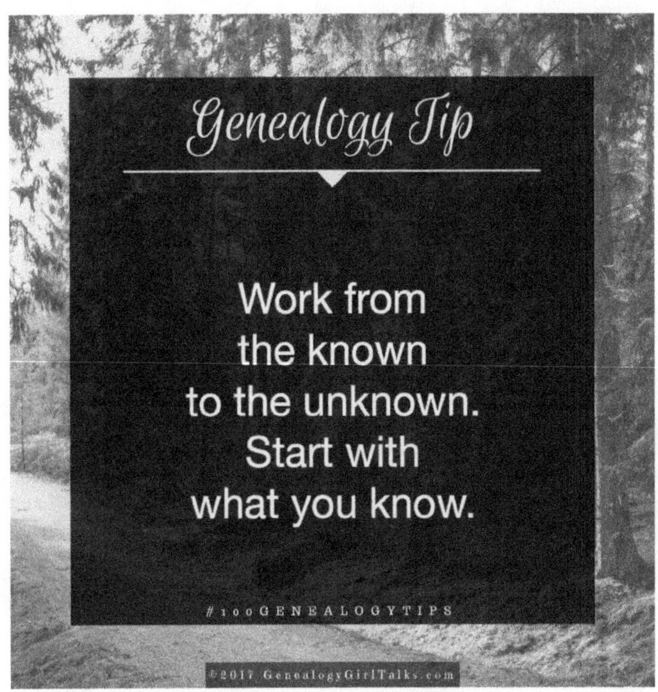
Genealogy Tip

Work from
the known
to the unknown.
Start with
what you know.

#100GENEALOGYTIPS

©2017 GenealogyGirlTalks.com

88. DNA Testing

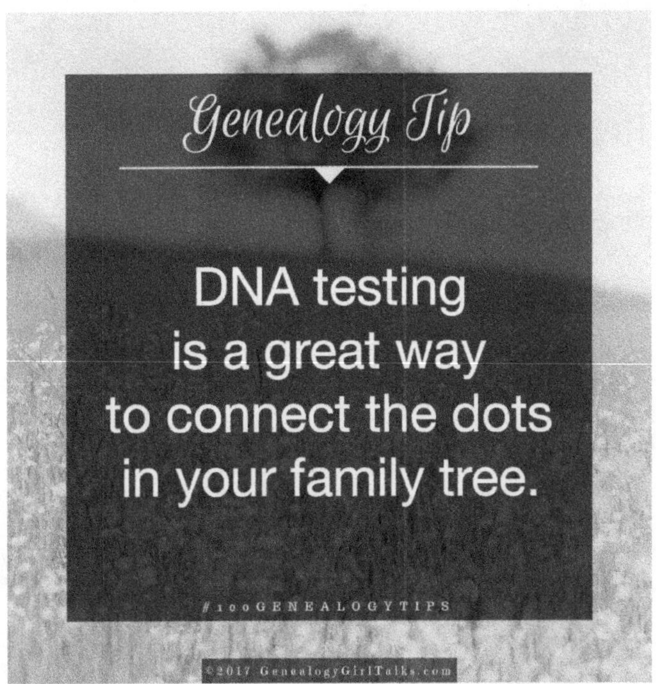

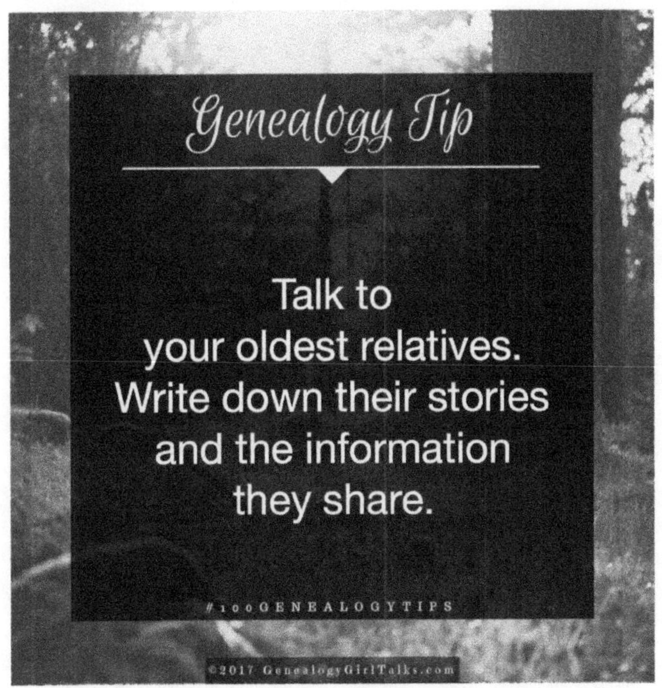
Genealogy Tip

Talk to
your oldest relatives.
Write down their stories
and the information
they share.

#100GENEALOGYTIPS

©2017 GenealogyGirlTalks.com

90. Mix Of Emotions

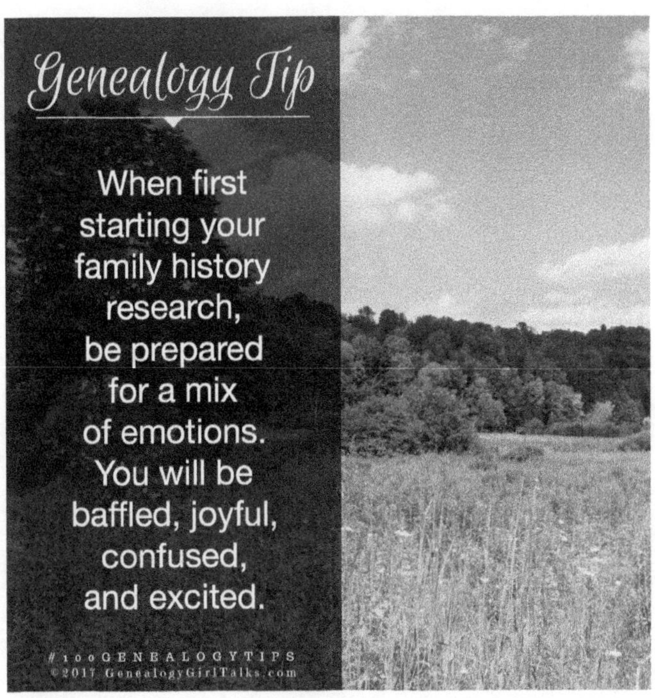

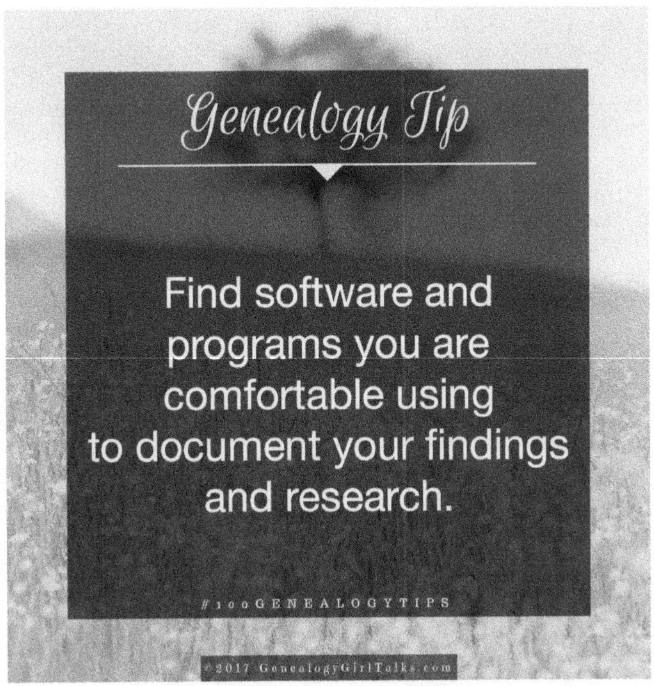

Genealogy Tip

Find software and
programs you are
comfortable using
to document your findings
and research.

#100GENEALOGYTIPS

© 2017 GenealogyGirlTalks.com

Genealogy Tip

Are you new
to family history research?
Wondering where to start?
Simply find a method
to document
your findings
and jump right in.

#100GENEALOGYTIPS

2017 GenealogyGirlTalks.com

Genealogy Tip
Expect
the
unexpected.
#100GENEALOGYTIPS
©2017 GenealogyGirlTalks.com

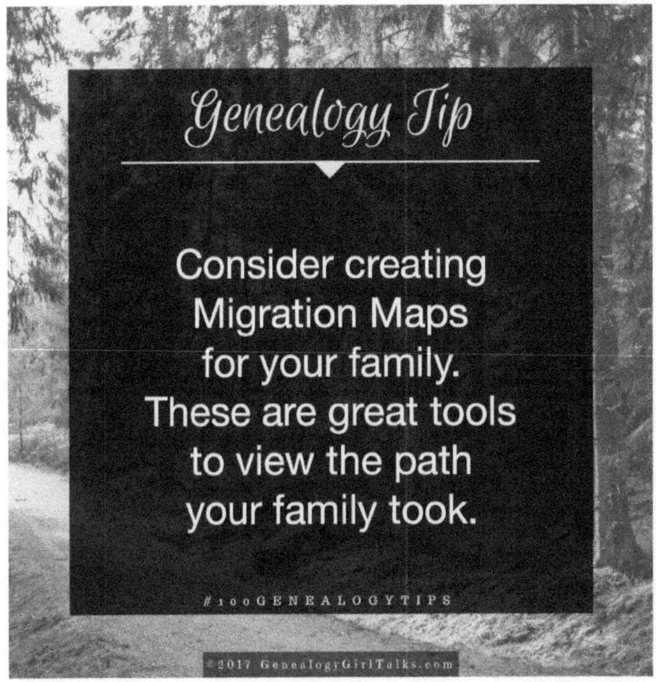
Genealogy Tip

Consider creating
Migration Maps
for your family.
These are great tools
to view the path
your family took.

#100GENEALOGYTIPS

©2017 GenealogyGirlTalks.com

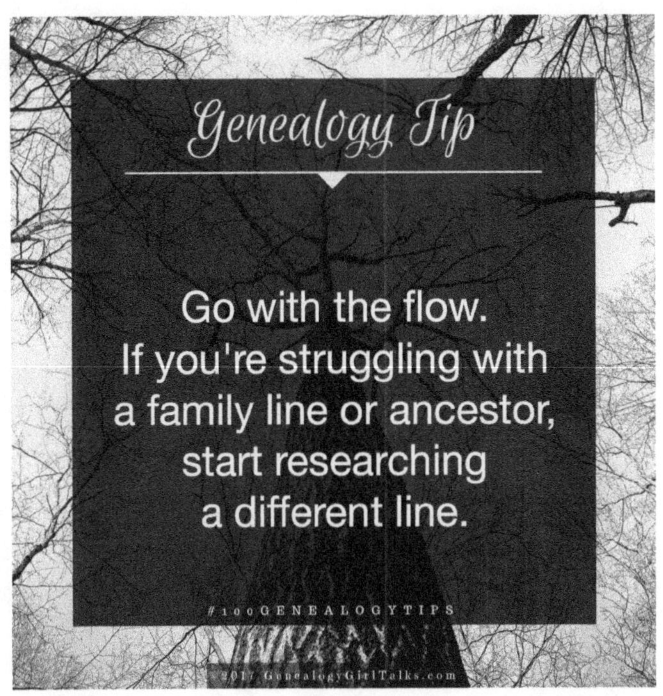
Genealogy Tip

Go with the flow.
If you're struggling with
a family line or ancestor,
start researching
a different line.

#100GENEALOGYTIPS
2017 GenealogyGirlTalks.com

Genealogy Tip

Create a Memorial
on Find A Grave
for your ancestors.
Add pictures and a
short biography.

#100GENEALOGYTIPS

©2017 GenealogyGirlTalks.com

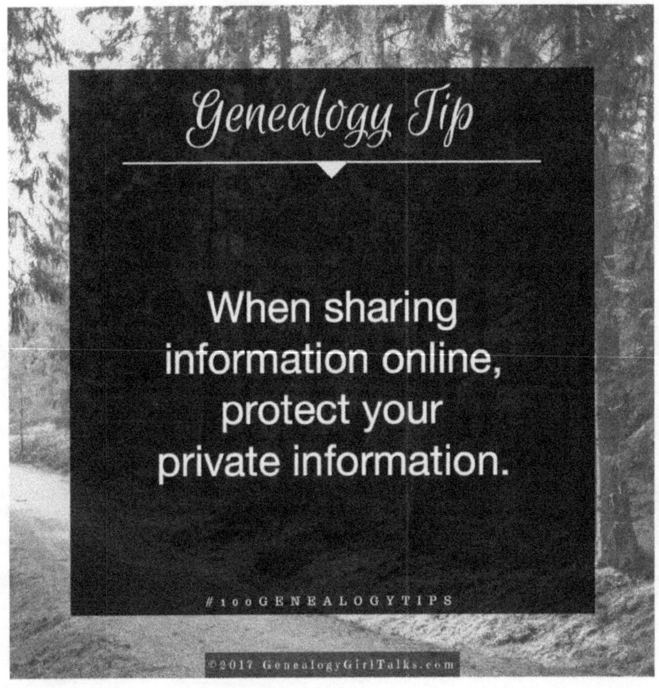
Genealogy Tip

When sharing
information online,
protect your
private information.

#100GENEALOGYTIPS

©2017 GenealogyGirlTalks.com

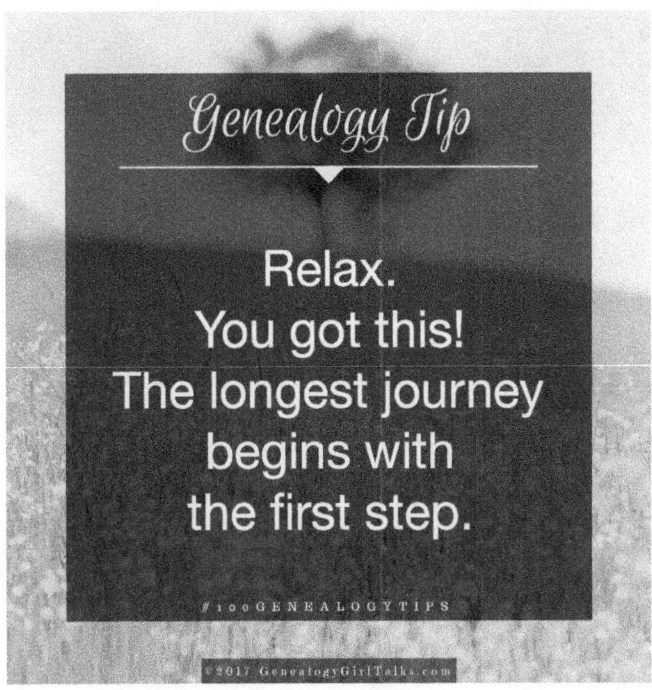
Genealogy Tip

Relax.
You got this!
The longest journey
begins with
the first step.

#100GENEALOGYTIPS

©2017 GenealogyGirlTalks.com

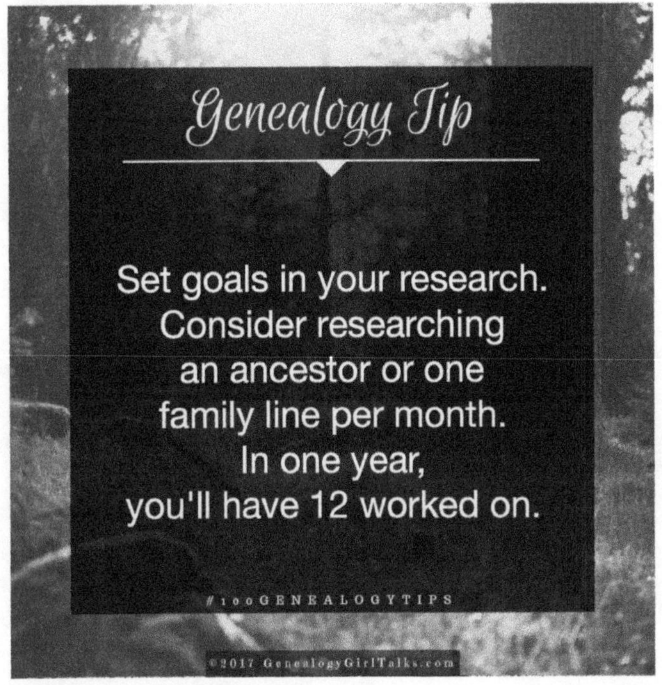
Genealogy Tip

Set goals in your research.
Consider researching
an ancestor or one
family line per month.
In one year,
you'll have 12 worked on.

#100GENEALOGYTIPS

©2017 GenealogyGirlTalks.com

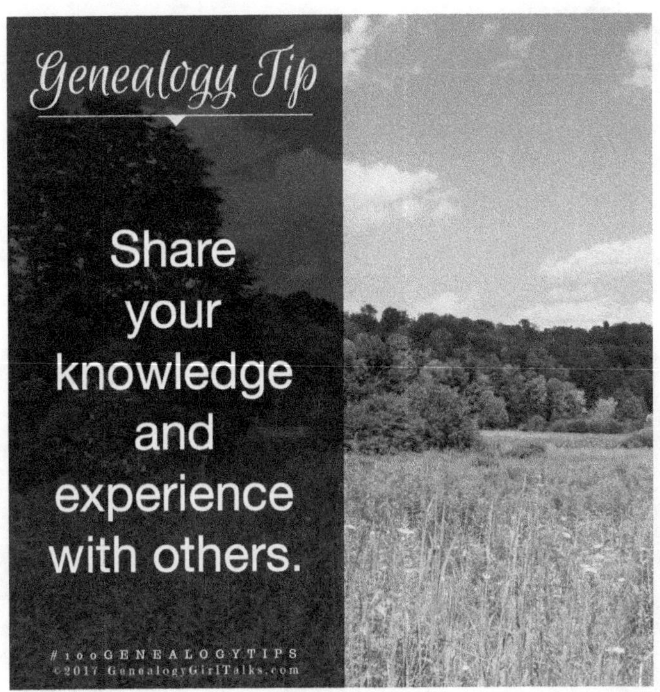

Genealogy Tip
Share your knowledge and experience with others.
#100GENEALOGYTIPS
©2017 GenealogyGirlTalks.com

ABOUT THE AUTHOR

Melissa Dickerson, also known as "Genealogy Girl Talks" has been conducting family history and genealogy research for over twenty years. She has a love of history, family, teaching, and creativity. Those four passions pushed her to create Genealogy Girl Talks in 2014.

She wrote her first eBook, "10 Tips for Using Pinterest for Family History" in the Fall 2014. That was followed by several more quick tip eBooks. In May 2016, her first print book was self-published ("Using Pinterest for Family History and Genealogy").

Melissa lives in Northeast Ohio, but her roots find her deep in pursuit of her family history in Appalachia. Her burning desire to learn more about her family and her roots in Southwestern West Virginia has quickly become her life's pursuit.

You can find Melissa at www.GenealogyGirlTalks.com and on various social media platforms. Follow the links on the website!